# THE CIVIL WAR COOKBOOK

## WILLIAM C. DAVIS

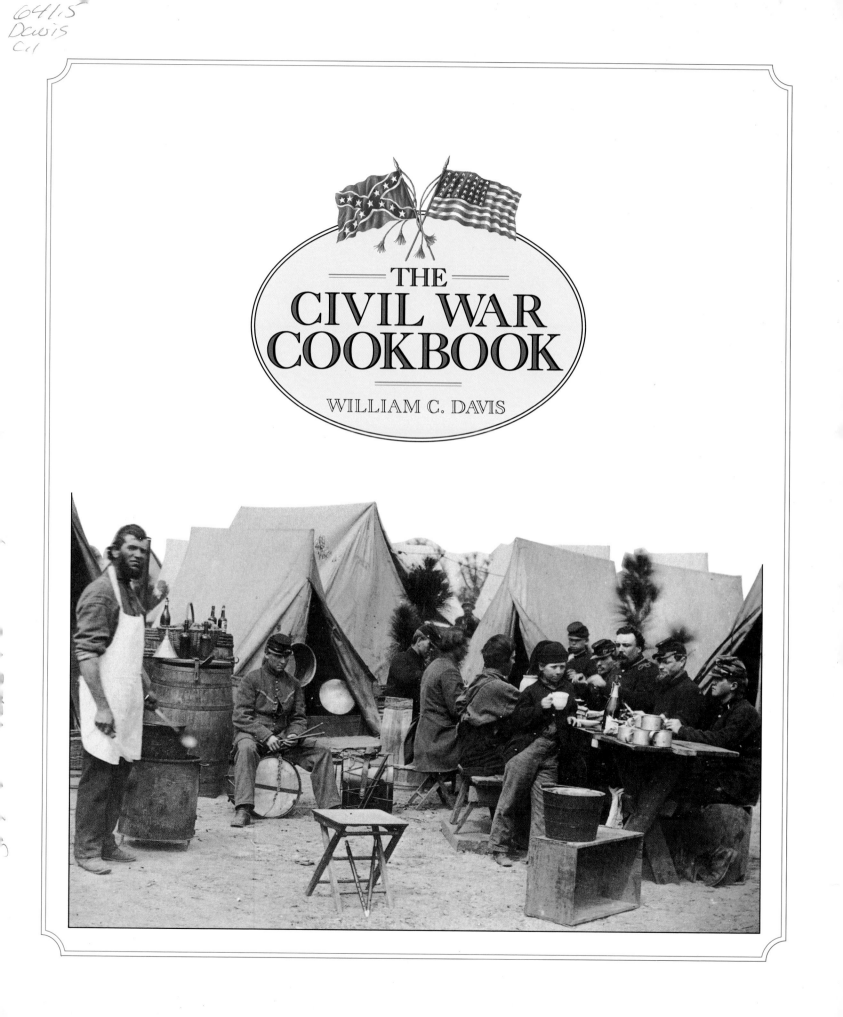

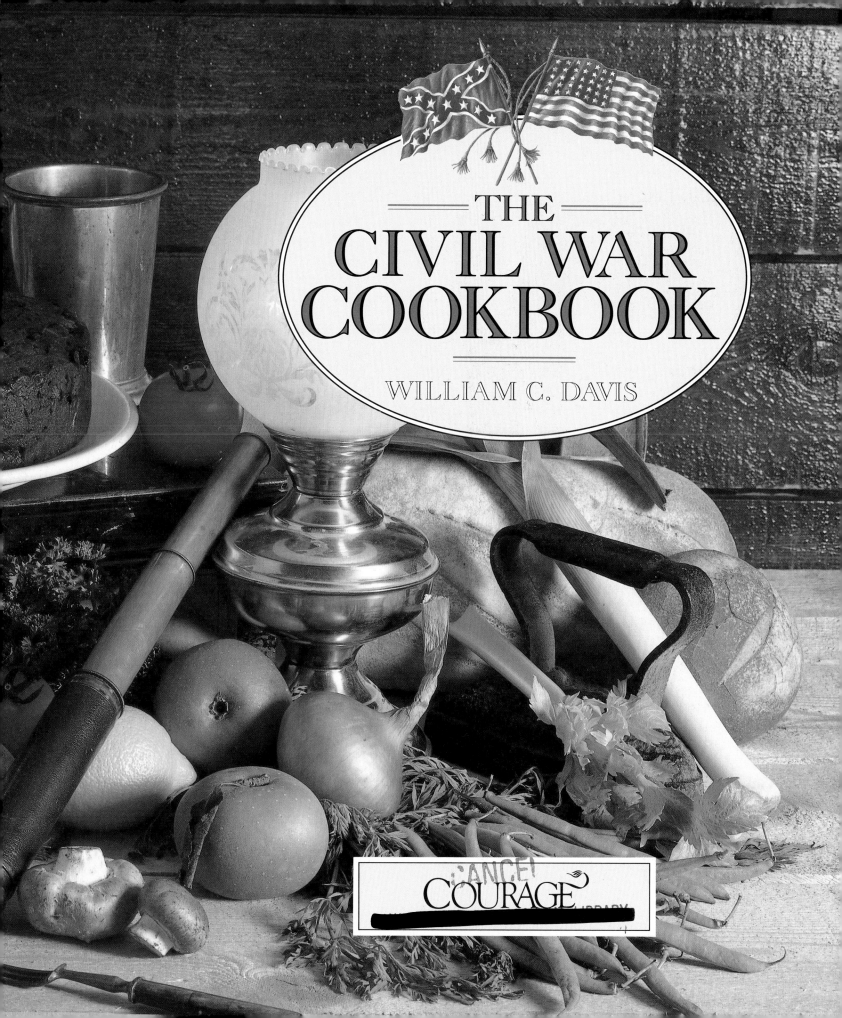

# THE CIVIL WAR COOKBOOK

## WILLIAM C. DAVIS

COURAGE

*Right: a wealthy officer has his servants perform routine tasks such as cleaning his sword and cooking a meal. The comforts afforded to officers were very different from that of the enlisted men.*

CLB 2924
9 8 7 6 5 4 3 2
Digit on the right indicates the number of this printing.

Library of Congress Cataloging-in-Publication Number 93-070599

ISBN 1-56138-287-6

This book was designed and produced by CLB Publishing, Godalming, Surrey, England.

Editor: Jillian Stewart
Designers: Stonecastle Graphics
Picture Researcher: Leora Kahn
Art Director: Roger Hyde
Photographers: Peter Barry and Neil Sutherland

Typesetting by Julie Smith
Printed and bound in Italy

Published by Courage Books,
an imprint of Running Press Book Publishers
125 South Twenty-second Street
Philadelphia, Pennsylvania 19103

# Contents

# Introduction

*Above: eating was the most important activity in
camp as it gave a sense of structure to the day.*

"The cooking is everything," said General Silas Casey in
1862. "If not well done it is positively injurious; if well
done, it is wholesome."

That yankee general was a bit ahead of his time in
even paying any attention at all to one of the most
essential elements in warfare. For generations military
men had bandied about the maxim that an army
marched "on its stomach," but few, if any, thought
beyond the expression. Governments and commanders
largely assumed that their culinary responsibility
extended only so far as obtaining basic supplies and
distributing them to the men in the field. After that, how
the men prepared and ate their fare, what they used to
supplement their rations, and indeed even the basic
nutritional requirements of a man in the field, were up
very much to the individual, or to the officers and non-
commissioned officers immediately above him.

*Right: smoking was one of the soldier's chief pleasures.*

Consequently, neither Union nor Confederate forces went into the field with standard manuals of cookery, nor with anything like an idea of proper food sanitation and handling. The whole science of nutrition had not yet been born. Manuals for quartermasters and commissaries were adopted by the respective war departments, but again, these extended only so far as the proper ration to be issued to the man in uniform, and that ration had not changed materially since the days of the Revolution. In the Northern forces, it was to consist <u>ideally</u> of:

*¾lb pork or bacon, or 1¼lbs of fresh or salt beef*
*18oz of flour or bread, or 12oz of hardtack,*
*or 11¼lbs of corn meal*

plus a daily issue to each 100 man company of:

*8 quarts of peas or beans, or 10 lbs rice*
*6-10 lbs of coffee, or 1½lbs of tea*
*12-15 lbs of sugar*
*4 quarts of vinegar*
*2 quarts of salt*

Fruit, fresh vegetables, dairy products, especially milk, were entirely absent. This did not mean that the commissaries thought that men did not need such essentials: only that the governments could not undertake to provide them on a regular basis, therefore excluding them from the prescribed ration. "A judicious use of

*Above: enjoying a drink near Fortress Monroe, Virginia.*

the ration," concluded Casey, "will furnish a diet of considerable variety, which may be still further extended by the purchase, from the company fund, of vegetables, butter, milk etc." It was up to the men themselves, or their officers, to find such things in their locality.

The military authorities' attitude toward what the men ate and how they prepared it was largely a reflection of the time in which they lived. Soldiers dined on much the same raw materials as they had when at home on their farms. Meat was the staple of almost every diet, and they ate it either freshly killed, or preserved by a variety of means from pickling in brine, to smoked, dried, sugar cured, and even canned in tins. Vegetables and fruit were the other mainstays, eaten fresh when available, or else dried. Flour and rice provided the grain in the diet, with bread being ubiquitous on every table. Milk, butter, eggs, and cheeses rounded out the basic foodstuffs in the larders of virtually every American family of the time.

Cooking techniques of the time were basic, and had changed little, if at all, from the age-old methods brought to the New World from the Old. Meat was roasted, fried, or most often boiled, frequently in stews with the vegetables. Heavy steamed or boiled "puddings" were popular ways of cooking meats and vegetables in pastry. Vegetables themselves, if cooked, were almost invariably laced with pork or bacon fat for flavor, while seasoning on all dishes usually extended little farther than salt and pepper and a few fresh herbs like bay leaf. Desserts, too, were closer related to European – especially English – fashion than to what Americans of the next century would adopt. Fruit pies, especially apple and cherry, were universally popular. Cakes, however, were generally of the very heavy and moist fruit cake variety, laced with fruits, nuts, and liquor, and capable of lasting for weeks or longer. Suet puddings rounded out the list of prepared desserts, with lighter delectables like cream pies and sponge, or layer cakes, reserved only for special occasions, due to the fact that they could not travel well and would not keep.

Beyond this, regional variation was already showing its influence on American tables. The distinctive Creole cuisine of southern Louisiana was well established. The "burgoo" stews and barbecues of the backwoods of Tennessee and Kentucky excited the palates of native sons, while Virginia ham, Boston beans, and New England chowders, all stood out in the fare of their localities.

Moreover, recent technological developments made it possible by 1860 for some of these regional specialties to be enjoyed elsewhere. Smoking, pickling, and drying, were preservation techniques older than human memory. But within this century men had discovered the art of vacuum packing meats and vegetables in tin cans and glass jars. The Hormel company was already making tinned meats available commercially. Gail Borden had recently developed a process for "condensing" milk, putting it in tins that could keep it for months. And others had found a method for shrinking and dehydrating vegetables, allowing them to keep for long periods before adding water caused them to swell again in cooking; making a palatable, if uninspiring, dish.

Thus when war erupted in April 1861 and thousands of young men flocked to the colors, means were at least available to get food to them, while their own experience at home had taught them a few rudimentary cookery skills to convert the raw rations into something edible, though not always either nourishing or healthful. Still there was much to learn, for in a regiment of 1,000 men, each might have his own idea of what to eat and how to make it. Thus a uniformity quickly spread through the camp kitchens, imposed in part by the limitations of what was provided, as well as by instructions from officers, particularly the commissary of subsistence. "Army food" was army food, then as later, and if the officials did not go to great lengths to prescribe exactly how to make it, still the authorities knew what they expected their men to eat, however prepared.

"Bread and soup are the great items of a soldier's diet in every situation," declared one general; "to make them well is therefore an essential part of a cook's instruction." Indeed bread was the one indispensable feature of the soldier's fare, though "bread" in army terms could mean many things. For North and South, the term "army bread" meant, in fact, hardtack – a thick soda cracker or biscuit about three inches square and perhaps half an inch thick. Private bakers made it to army contracts and shipped it in endless crates to the men in the field. "Sheet iron teeth dullers," some called it, with trenchant reference to the incredible hardness of the cracker. Noting how often the biscuits arrived infested with maggots, others dubbed them "worm castles." It was a brave man who could chew through one. Some

*Above: Lt. Bostwick and Lt. Babcock of the 7th New York.*

authorities, old soldiers themselves, understood. "Hard bread will be more palatable and more easy of digestion if placed in...ashes until thoroughly heated," suggested Captain Robert Scott of the 4th United States Infantry. "It can also be improved by breaking it in pieces an inch or two square and soaking it thoroughly in warm water, then placing it in a frying pan with a few slices of pork and cooked for five minutes, stirring it that all may be cooked alike." In fact, this is how most men ate hardtack. They crushed the crackers under their rifle butts and either soaked the bits in water, or else fried them directly in a thick layer of grease or pork fat, sometimes adding meat if they had it.

Soft fresh bread was far preferable, and usually available except when on the march, if army bakers were present. These seem to be the only specialized cooks in the service, and they worked on a large scale indeed, especially in the Union army. Baking bread was neither a quick or an easy task. They started with the yeast, putting three handfuls of hops into a large kettle of boiling water. Some of the hop water was then worked into a paste with four pounds of flour, and the balance of the hop mixture added when thoroughly boiled. Then three pints of crushed malt went into the mixture along with two quarts of what they called "start yeast." All that had to sit for fifteen hours, and when strained it provided a bubbling mass ready to make a dough rise.

Even the dough was a complicated process. First it required a "ferment." One and one-half pecks of potatoes were boiled with their skins on, then mixed into six pounds of flour, six pails full of water and six quarts of the new "start yeast" were added to complete the ferment. Made at night, it was allowed to sit until morning when, after straining, three and one-half pails full of it were worked into a dough with nine and a half barrels of flour, three and one-half pounds of salt, and four pails of hot water. After thorough kneading it was set aside for two hours to "prove," then kneaded once more "by throwing it in masses on to the table." Only

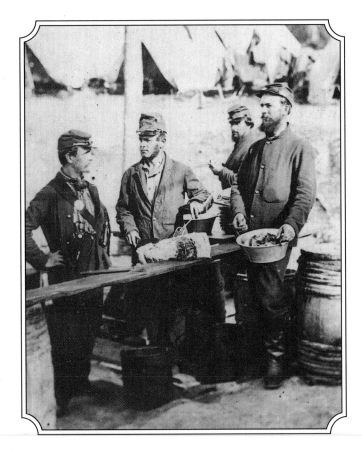

*Above: preparing the meat for the next meal.*

then was it ready to be cut into loaves and baked in huge trays for about fifty minutes. Just one such batch of dough would make 288 loaves! It may not have come out as good as mother's back home, but when available it was a blissfully soft and tasty alternative to hardtack. For Confederates, to whom wheat flour was not often available, cornbread or "pone" was a replacement, though hardly a good substitute. Corn meal was far too prone to weevils, and improperly cooked pone too quickly turned moldy, or else became too stale to eat. As a result, Johnny Rebs treated it in much the same way as they did hardtack. They crumbled the pone into their skillets, added the ubiquitous grease and perhaps some peas, and fried it into a thick glutinous mess called "cush."

Soup, that other staple of the soldier's diet, was less complex, and offered much more variety. "Soup cannot be too highly esteemed," said General Casey. "It should be used more often than it is," though he added the culinary touch that "great care should be taken to boil it slowly and for a long time." Good beef soup was to combine rice, fresh vegetables, "desiccated" (dehydrated) vegetables, and of course beef, along with the bones, cooked at least five hours with the rice, with the rice going in half an hour before serving. Bean soup, which Captain Scott thought "when properly made is one of the best that can be used," required steeping the dried beans in water overnight, then putting over the fire at reveille for six hours, adding one-third ration per man of pork, three hours before eating. "This eaten with a little pepper and vinegar, makes a wholesome and palatable [sic] dish."

"All fried meats are unwholesome." So stated General Casey, though he probably did not know it was the excessive slurry of grease that made men ill. For eating beef, rather, Casey prescribed that it be cooked on coals, suspended from a stick or fork, which was indeed the preferred method when a frying pan was not handy. The same was true for pork, though many liked to boil salt pork for several hours, then slice it when cold and take it with a piece of bread and a slice of onion. Stews provided another more tasty way of cooking meat. Beef was cut into chunks, with potatoes, desiccated vegetables, onion, some small pieces of pork, and salt and pepper to taste. Stewed slowly in water for three hours, General Casey stated "this will make an excellent dish."

Vegetables presented challenges of their own. "Every cook thinks he can cook potatoes," said Captain Scott, "but few can cook them well." He advised boiling them in water until nearly done, then pouring off the liquid and standing the kettle over the fire until it stopped steaming, throwing in a handful of salt. As for the infamous desiccated vegetables, all sorts of stories had arisen. Soldiers called the dried cakes "bales of hay," and told tall tales of men who had made the mistake of eating them dry, only to swell until they exploded as the dehydrated stuff expanded in their stomachs. "Desiccated vegetables should be thoroughly cooked," said Scott. "The want of this has given rise to an unfounded prejudice against them. It is the fault of the cooking and not of the vegetables."

Beans were also a preferred dish, especially in the Navy. General Casey even had a recipe for "left-overs" from the previous day's bean soup, suggesting that they be warmed with some previously sautéed onion on top of them, along with pepper, salt, and a tablespoon of vinegar. Hominy was also common, especially in the Confederacy, and dried peaches and apples, when stewed, "are desirable articles." A sprinkling of ginger or clove added nicely to them, making "a valuable store to be used occasionally," said General Casey.

Finally there was coffee. Soldiers could go for days without food, if only they had their coffee. In the Confederacy it became as highly prized as shoes, and commanded outrageous prices in times of scarcity. Substitutes were tried using chicory or parched corn, but nothing approached the real article. As a result, coffee was the item most often requested when Rebs informally met Yanks between the lines for illicit trading; Virginia tobacco being the commodity exchanged. In the North, by contrast, there was rarely any shortage of coffee beans, and many regiments were actually issued special rifles, one per 100-man company, with a coffee grinder built into the butt stock. The best coffee was slow roasted over a low fire "until of a chestnut brown color and not burnt, as is so commonly done." It was to be boiled briskly for two minutes, then taken from the fire at once, a little cold water thrown in, then the boiler's contents poured through a piece of flannel after it had settled for five minutes.

In the end, the fighting men ate what they could get, and cooked it in whatever means was most convenient,

*Above: returning to Camp Reynolds after a successful foraging mission.*

or most tasty. The ingredients and methods suggested by Casey, Scott and others may have predominated, but when men were left so much to their own devices, innovation and improvisation, especially in the Confederacy, became a way of life. A group of Confederates in South Carolina made a meal of rats, finding that "rat tasted like young squirrel." Another recounted how "I overcame prejudice against the bull frog and found him very nice." Dogs, cats, even mules, went into stew pots. At Vicksburg, Mississippi, for years after the war, it was said that the city was rat free. The starving Confederate garrison during the 1863 siege had caught and eaten them all, even publishing recipes in the local newspaper.

Those were hardships sometimes shared by soldier and civilian alike in a war that often blurred the distinctions of people in and out of uniform. The experience was no culinary lark, and was not so intended. Men ate to live, and lived to fight, and if their fare was not extravagant, still the heavy diet gave them protein, starch, and animal fats, to provide the energy needed for days of endless marching and the feverish heat of battle.

# CHAPTER ONE

# Off to War

*Above: the camp kitchens offered raw recruits a very different experience from their last meal at home!*

Regardless of what lay ahead of them in war, virtually every man who donned the Blue or Gray shared at least one common experience: the exciting, perhaps tearful, perhaps a little fearful, departure from home. "Our enlisting was like many other things in this world," wrote one Maine volunteer. "One started and the rest thoughtlessly followed." Mothers weepily prepared the grandest going-away meals that the larder would allow, assuming their boys had not run away to enlist. The fatted calf was killed or a prime hog butchered, pies made, jellies and relishes brought out of the pantry, cakes prepared, and undoubtedly the boy's favorite dishes were prepared for what all feared – yet none dared say – might be his last meal with the family.

*A soldier's farewell meal with his family was a far cry from what his next meal held in store for him. A Confederate's first meal as a soldier might be no better than Johnny Jackman's when he left home to join the Kentucky infantry, "a piece of fat bacon on the end of a stick, and ... a fragment of cornbread."*

*Right: Wm. McKinley enlisting in the army (1861). He survived the Civil War only to be assassinated in 1901.*

*Below: cased ambrotypes of loved ones were one of the few personal possessions soldiers carried with them.*

# Bean Soup

*Beans were an important source of protein during the war, and sustained many a hungry soldier deprived of fresh meat and dairy produce.*

$^1/_2$ *pound uncooked navy beans*
$^3/_4$ *pound ham shank*
*1 cup diced potatoes (uncooked)*
$^3/_4$ *cup diced onion*
*3 large tomatoes, skinned and finely chopped*
*Salt and pepper*
*1 Tbsp parsley*

*Cover the beans with cold water and soak overnight. Rinse the beans, cover with fresh water, cook until tender and then strain. Cover the ham with cold water and simmer until tender, skimming off the fat. Add the beans, potatoes, and onion to the ham and simmer gently. When the vegetables are almost tender, add the tomatoes, salt and pepper, and parsley, and cook slowly until the vegetables are ready. The soup can be served immediately but tastes better reheated on the following day. Serves 6.*

*Right: leaving for war was a time of mixed emotions for both the soldiers and their loved ones.*

*Right: the anguish of departure is evocatively portrayed in this 1861 painting entitled "Their Country's Call," by J.L.G. Ferris.*

# Bouilli

*One pot meals were common during the period as they utilized whatever ingredients were available, and, of course, they were very simple to cook. This authentic recipe from a cookbook of the time is very basic by our standards.*

*To a tender piece of beef, (about ten pounds,) put three pints of water, a little pepper, salt, and an onion. Boil the beef gently for three or four hours; the beef should be turned, and the water renewed as it boils away. Crumbs of bread should be put in to thicken the gravy.*

*About half an hour before it is to be taken up, the fat should be carefully skimmed off, then a little cabbage, carrots, turnips, and celery, cut small, are to be put in, and boiled until quite tender.*

# Pork Pie with Green Beans

*Filled pies were very plain, with a simple meat filling and the most basic paste (pastry) topping. The treatment given to vegetables was different from today – they were boiled with a piece of meat as this was thought to give them a better flavor!*

1 pound pork, chopped
Salt and pepper
Flour

6 Tbsps butter
1 Tbsp lard
2 cups flour
Pinch salt
Cold water

*Cover the pork with water and stew until tender. Remove the meat and flavor the remaining juices with the salt and pepper, thicken with a little flour and then set aside.*

*Rub the butter and lard into the flour, add the salt and mix in enough cold water to make a nice dough. Roll out dough and line a deep pie dish. Fill the dish with the cooked pork and cover with the gravy. Cover the meat with dough and bake until the paste is lightly browned.*

*Wash 1 pound green beans and remove the tops and tails. Cut into small lengths and place in a pot of boiling water. Boil for fifteen minutes, adding salt and pepper five minutes from end of cooking time. If available, bacon fat or pork was added before boiling to impart extra flavor. Serves 4*

*Below: such were the rigors of army life that few pieces of kitchen equipment remain from the period. Soldiers discarded any unnecessary utensils and carried only the bare essentials.*

*Top: bounties were used to entice the North's almost limitless supply of young men into the recruiting tents in New York's Central Park.*

Young Yankee boys going off to war fared little better than their southern counterparts. Indeed, one company of Maine recruits found that their captain had not even anticipated that they might need to eat until they reminded him. "He ordered his cook to furnish us with as good as the larder afforded," Private John Haley wrote in his diary that first night. "We were soon munching 'salt horse' and washing it down with copious draughts of some kind of tea which tasted strongly of turkey stuffing. We also had bread, accompanied by a villainous substance masquerading as butter," he continued. "It proved a sorry apology for the real thing, having the tokens of age and being tall-flavored."

*Right: a drawing by Charles W. Reed of a recruiting office. The artist himself later enlisted in the Ninth Massachusetts Battery.*

*Below: Midshipman Hardin B. Littlepage, who ably served one of the Virginia's guns.*

# Old-fashioned Meat Loaf

*Meat was an important part of the diet in both armies. Unfortunately, once actually leaving home for the war soldiers were more likely to receive an old piece of tough beef than the good home-cooked meat dishes they received at home.*

$^1/_2$ pound ground ham
$^1/_2$ pound sausage meat
Salt and pepper
4 Tbsps milk
1 egg
$^1/_2$ cup bread crumbs
$^1/_4$ cup water
1 tsp dry mustard

Mix ham and sausage meat together and season. Add the milk, egg, and bread crumbs, and mix thoroughly. Heat the water and add the mustard, bring to a boil and add to the meat mixture. Shape the loaf into a shallow baking pan and bake in a moderate oven (375° F) for about 1 hour. Serves 6-8.

*Above: canned vegetables, mustard and baking powder were available, but their quality and safety were dubious.*

## Carrot Pudding

*Boil six large carrots, strain them through a sieve, and add half a pound of butter, half a pint of cream, eight eggs, cinnamon, rose water, wine, and sugar to taste. Bake for one hour in a medium pie dish lined with paste (pastry).*

# Red Flannel Hash

*Soldiers may have eaten this hash at home, but it is certainly tastier than the version served to the army! Beets and fresh herbs add extra flavor, but add some of your own favorites, as this dish has always been concocted from any leftover ingredients which may have been on hand.*

*1 pound corned beef*
*4 large cold boiled potatoes, chopped*
*1 medium onion, finely chopped*
*Salt, pepper and nutmeg*
*1-2 cooked beets, peeled and diced*
*Fresh herbs to taste*
*2 Tbsps butter*

*Cut the beef into small pieces. Combine all the remaining ingredients except the butter. Melt the butter in a skillet and when foaming add the meat mixture. Spread the mixture out evenly in the pan. Cook over low heat, pressing the mixture down continuously with a wooden spoon or spatula. Cook for about 15-20 minutes. When a crust forms on the bottom, turn over and brown the other side. Cut into wedges and remove from the pan to serve. Serves 2-4.*

*Right: Brigadier General O.B. Willcox and his staff at Petersburg, August, 1864. Severely wounded and captured at Bull Run, he was later exchanged and fought through the Wilderness campaign as division commander.*

*Above: this comical wartime drawing shows the return of a foraging party of the Twenty-Fourth Regiment, Connecticut Volunteers complete with mules, wagons, and provisions.*

*Fortunately, to get them through the dreadful first days of soldiering, most mothers and girlfriends sent their boys off to war with hampers and boxes packed with home-baked goodies that, alas, lasted not nearly long enough as the recruits shared them with their messmates.*

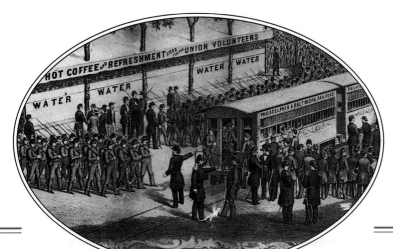

*Right: a lithograph by W. Boell portrays the citizens of Philadelphia welcoming the volunteer Union regiments with a Refreshment Saloon.*

*Above: the scars of battle are evident on the faces of brothers Frederick and Henry Cordes. The brothers were members of the Pennsylvania "Bucktails," regiments who wore deer tails in their hats.*

# Traditional Sally Lunn

*This light, sweet bread was named for the 18th-century English woman who first made it. Many recipes, or "receipts" as they were known, were reminiscent of cooking styles brought from the Old World.*

1 cup milk
2 Tbsps shortening
$\frac{1}{2}$ oz active dry yeast
3 cups flour
$\frac{1}{2}$ tsp salt
1 egg
1 Tbsp sugar

*Heat the milk and shortening to scalding point and then allow to cool. Pour the milk into a bowl, add the remaining ingredients and mix until smooth. Cover the bowl and leave in a warm place to rise for about 1-1$\frac{1}{2}$ hours. Knock down the dough and put in a greased pan and allow to rise for a further hour. Bake in a moderately hot oven (375° F) for about 45 minutes.*

## Cottage Cheese

*Among civilians this was a common way of using up old milk, but it would have seemed like an emperors dish to a hungry soldier.*

*If you have some milk which is turning sour, cover it and set aside in a warm place to curdle. When it becomes a curd, strain it to remove the liquid. Place the curd in a clean muslin bag and suspend it with the pointed end over a bowl. Put in a cool place for about 12 hours then remove the cheese and flavor it with a little cream and some butter.*

*The evening of his first day in camp, Johnny Jackman fell in with a friend who "fed me on pies and such things," leaving him to look back later at the war's end and reflect that "that was the best commissariat we ever had."*

*Above right: this woodcut from 1862 shows women preparing clothing for the soldiers while others urge their beaux to enlist*

## Apple Pie

*Apple desserts have always been popular where there is a good apple crop, but as the war dragged on even apples became scarce and many recipes for apple pie without apples appeared!*

*Below: Colonel Arthur Herbert of the 17th Virginia Infantry in typical Confederate field officer's dress.*

8 medium-sized greenings
(first apples of the harvest)
1 Tbsp butter
1 cup white sugar
$^1/_2$ cup culinary rose water
A little grated nutmeg
$^1/_2$ cup butter
2 cups flour
Pinch salt
Cold water

*Core the apples, chop coarsely and stew until softened – about 15 minutes. When done, add the butter, sugar, rose water, and nutmeg, and mix well.*

*Previous to making the apple filling, make the dough. Rub the butter into the flour, add the salt and mix in enough cold water to make a nice dough. Roll out enough dough to line a deep pie dish. Line the dish with the dough and fill with the apple mixture. Roll out the remaining dough and cover the dish. Glaze with beaten egg and bake for 30 minutes in a moderate oven (375° F).*

*Above: uniforms and personal clothing intermingled, especially in the Confederacy. Of the Yankee clothing above, worn in the first battle of Bull Run, only the kepi is regulation.*

# CHAPTER TWO

# Camp and Field

*Above: Blackburn's Ford, Bull Run, July 1862.*

*"Hd Qrs Provisional Brigades
Washington Nov. 19, 1862*

*The attention of those having charge of new troops cannot be too often called to the importance of seeing to the proper preparation of the food provided for the men under their command."*

*Unfortunately, too many officers failed to follow the good example set by General Silas Casey in prescribing that dictate to the men under his command.*

*In some commands, as in Casey's, two men from each 100-man company were detailed permanently, one as chief cook, and the other as assistant. In other outfits, the men did their cooking in 20-man squads, informally choosing their own cooks and often rotating the duty.*

*While both armies established and operated commissary departments to see to the acquisition and distribution of food stuffs to the men in the ranks, there was never any attempt to impose an orderly, uniform, or nutritious control over how such things were prepared.*

*Left: a sutler's store in front of Petersburg. In the early days of the war there were delays in paying the troops, and often a soldier would owe the sutler all his money by the time the paymaster arrived. Right: a reconstruction of a camp store.*

# Artificial Oysters

*This was a common meal in the South when food was scarce and only the most basic ingredients were available.*

*2 eggs*
*3/4 cup flour*
*Pinch of salt to taste*
*Pinch of pepper*
*2 cups of whole-kernel corn*

*Beat the eggs and add the flour gradually, mixing until smooth. Add the seasoning and corn; mix thoroughly. If the mixture is too thick, add a little water. Separate the mixture into balls and flatten into oyster shapes. Heat some oil in a skillet and fry the "oysters" until slightly brown on both sides. Makes 6.*

*Above right: camp life often involved men cooking for themselves in small groups. Unfortunately, this often meant poor use of already poor ingredients.*

*Above: Confederate battlefield artifacts are particularly rare and show the diversity of weapons used, from the ancient battered pistol to the roughly-made saber and the brightly handled knife.*

# Rabbit Stew

*Fresh meat was greatly prized throughout the war, and for a hungry soldier deprived of good rations, rabbit or squirrel was a very acceptable alternative to beef and pork.*

*1 rabbit, dressed and cut into pieces*
*1/4 cup flour*
*Salt and pepper*
*Piece of butter size of an egg (4 Tbsps)*
*2 onions*
*3/4 cup chopped carrots*
*1 cup coarsely chopped potatoes*
*Mixed herbs*

*Mix the flour and seasoning together, and coat the rabbit in the mixture. Melt the butter and fry the rabbit pieces to brown. Put the pieces in a large pan and add the onion, carrot, and potato. Cover with water and season with salt, pepper, and herbs. Cover and cook in a moderate oven (375° F) for about 1 hour. Serves 2-3*

*Below: charity organisations such as the U.S. Sanitary Commission provided cups and other essential items for the soldiers' day-to-day use.*

*With neither official cookery books nor nutritional guides to assist them, the soldiers had to depend on their own ingenuity or their officer's conscientiousness. General Casey required inspections of kettles and kitchens to be made daily, to ensure that utensils were kept clean, further advising that "care should be taken to vary the diet as much as possible, for sameness of diet, when long continued, weakens digestion."*

*Below: wine, beer, and spirit containers from the war. Soldiers showed remarkable ingenuity in obtaining liquor as there was no official ration in either army.*

*Left: a wartime drawing by Winslow Homer shows Union soldiers capturing livestock on a foraging mission. Below: camp cooks prepare another meal in the endless struggle to feed a hungry army.*

# Hash

*The beef or "salt horse" supplied to the army was of very poor quality and the men would mix and fry it with other ingredients to make it edible. Butter is used in this recipe, but soldiers would have used any fat they could obtain.*

*3 Tbsps butter or oil*
*³/₄ pound beef, cubed*
*1 large onion, diced*
*1 pound potatoes, cooked and diced*
*Salt and pepper*
*Water*

*Heat the butter or oil and fry the beef and onion until the beef is well browned. Add the cooked potatoes, salt, and pepper. Add enough water to make a pliable mixture and stir, breaking up the potatoes. Form the mixture into balls and flatten to about an inch thick. Fry the rounds on both sides until golden brown.*

*Right: a posed picture of a soldier's typical meal. The diet of a regular soldier was a very meager one. On the march, in particular, he was restricted to a ration that consisted mainly of salted meat, hardtack, potatoes, and coffee (if he was lucky).*

*Below: among a soldiers most treasured possessions were his eating and cooking utensils. A knife, fork, and spoon were sometimes carried, but the spoon-fork, spoon-knife combination was much more common.*

# Salt Pork

Salted meat was a crucial part of the diet in both armies. Salt pork in particular was common as it did not spoil and it was certainly preferable to the leather-like texture of salted beef. In civilian life too, pork was eaten by all sections of society with the wealthy adding herbs and spices to improve the flavor.

Preparing the pork was a lengthy business. The meat was carefully sectioned as soon as possible after the animal had been killed. Saltpetre (rock salt) was then rubbed into the meat and it was laid in a tub of salt. The meat was then left in this manner for about four weeks. After this time it was put into the smokehouse until it reached the stage when the meat would lift easily away from the bone.

*Above: hardtack was the army's equivalent of bread. A thick, unbelievably hard soda cracker, it had to be heated or soaked in warm water to make it edible.*

# Catfish Soup

· This authentic recipe uses very basic ingredients, but you can add your own favorite flavor enhancers.

¼ pound bacon
2 large onions, chopped
1 celery stalk, sliced
2 carrots, chopped
2 pounds catfish fillets, cut into large chunks
1 Tbsp chopped parsley
Salt and pepper
Water
3 eggs
1 Tbsp butter
2 Tbsps flour
1 cup milk

Fry the bacon in a Dutch oven until crisp. Remove bacon and reserve. Add the onions, celery, and carrots to the pan and fry until soft. Add fish, parsley, and seasoning, and enough water just to cover. Simmer until the fish is tender, but not breaking up. Mix together the eggs, butter, flour, and the milk. Heat the mixture and add to the soup along with the cooked bacon. Heat the soup gently until thickened, adjust seasoning and serve. Serves 4.

# Fricassee of Chicken

Officers fared better than most in the army, although this traditional fricassee would be considered very bland by today's highly flavored tastes.

2 medium-sized chickens
Salt and pepper
Piece of butter size of an egg (4 Tbsps)
$\frac{1}{2}$ cup flour
1 cup milk
$\frac{1}{2}$ cup white wine

Cut the chicken into breasts, legs and wings. Fill a pan with enough water to cover the chicken pieces, bring the pan to a boil, lower the heat and add the chicken pieces along with the salt and pepper. Simmer until tender – about 25-30 minutes. Reserve the cooking liquid as stock. Melt the butter gently and stir in the flour. Heat slowly for a minute then stir in the milk and $\frac{1}{2}$ cup of the chicken stock. Stir carefully for a few minutes and then stir in the wine. Add the chicken pieces and heat through. Adjust the seasoning to taste before serving. Serves 4-6.

*When cooking was left to the men themselves, orderliness, punctuality, and sanitation were forgotten all too often. Virtually everything was fried in a skillet in grease. Given the haphazard nature of food preservation at the time, much of what was issued to the men was already of indifferent quality. The way they went on to prepare it only made it worse, accounting for much of the widespread dysentery in both armies.*

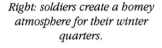

*Right: soldiers create a homey atmosphere for their winter quarters.*

*Below: the ubiquitous hardtack. Much hated by soldiers, but one of the few rations they could be sure to receive.*

# Cornbread

*The cornbread we eat today bears only a passing resemblance to that eaten during the Civil War years. In those days it was bland and rather tasteless, so add a little sugar to this traditional recipe if you feel the need.*

1/2 cup yellow cornmeal
1 cup flour
Pinch of salt
4 eggs
2 Tbsps milk
3 Tbsps butter, softened

*Combine the cornmeal, flour, and salt in a bowl. Add the eggs, milk, and butter and mix well. Pour into a 9 x 9-inch buttered baking pan and bake in a moderate oven (375° F) for 15-20 minutes.*

## Johnny Cakes

*There are many different recipes for Johnny or Journey Cakes, this original recipe is one of the simplest, and most authentic!*

*A quart of Indian meal mixed with a teaspoon of salt, scalded well with boiling water and baked about half an inch thick. When done, split through the middle, cut in pieces for the table and dip in butter.*

*Above: a soldier's footwear was fundamental to his well being. Boots were often ill-fitting and were the cause of great misery on long marches.*

46

# Indian Pudding

*Old-fashioned puddings were heavy and filling, and although it was a lucky soldier who received such a treat from the camp kitchen, they could often be put together from the most basic of ingredients if only there was some sugar to be had.*

3 cups milk
$^{1}/_{2}$ cup yellow cornmeal
$^{1}/_{4}$ tsp ground ginger
$^{1}/_{2}$ tsp salt
$^{1}/_{2}$ cup dark molasses
Piece of butter the size of a small egg (3 Tbsps)
1 egg, well beaten

*Bring the milk to a boil and slowly stir in the cornmeal. Add the ginger and salt and continue to heat for about 15 minutes until the cornmeal has thickened. Add the molasses, butter, and egg. Mix well and pour into a buttered baking dish. Bake in a moderate oven (350° F) for about 40 minutes. Serve the pudding warm, with whipped cream. Serves 2-4*

# CHAPTER THREE

# Dining Out

*Above: officers take advantage of a quiet moment to enjoy a leisurely meal.*

"*T*he remembrance of that wonderful kitchen hospitality will ever be a green spot in my experience." That was what Virginia cavalryman Issac Coles felt years after he and five comrades were entertained by an old couple for dinner in their home one winter evening during the war.

*"That tidy, genial most marvellous kitchen was like a dream … it's pans shone like mirrors, its crockery glistened." Never could he forget "the kindly face and portly outline of Mrs Beveridge as she stood by the stove frying buckwheat cakes for her country's hungry soldiers." I never knew such an expert and a magical cook," he went on. "I can see the agile movement of her arm as she flopped those appetizing cakes over into the pan and onto the plates." Better yet the cakes were covered with "real mountain syrup." "Such comfort, such undreamed of luxury," recalled Coles, "we were not to know again for many an ill day."*

*Comforts and luxuries were rare for the soldier in Blue or Gray. Yet, when they went out singly or in small groups of two or three, they might sometimes find an agreeable farmer's wife willing to treat them to something sweetly different from their usual army fare.*

*Right: the daughters of Maryland refresh Union soldiers with food and water as they march against the Confederate invaders.*

*Below: reading material was important to all soldiers, and news vendors visited both armies selling magazines, newspapers, and the popular illustrated newspapers.*

# Tomato Soup

*This tomato soup is very different from the pureed versions we eat today, but it would be welcome change from army food for a soldier lucky enough to find a family of sympathizers willing to feed him.*

Piece of beef with bone in
6 cups water
12 tomatoes, skinned and coarsely chopped
2 small onions, chopped
Salt and pepper
Thyme, tarragon and marjoram to taste
1 bay leaf

*Place the piece of beef in a saucepan with the water and bring to the boil. Skim the surface and add remaining ingredients. Simmer for about 1½ hours then remove bay leaf and meat. Taste and adjust seasoning, adding a little sugar if the soup is bitter. Serves 4.*

*Unfortunately, as the years dragged on and the countryside was increasingly ravaged by foraging armies, the willingness of private citizens to show hospitality, even to friendly troops, diminished.*

*Right: an engraving by W.H. Shelton of General Duke testing the pies.*

*Below: a soldier's typical mess equipment consisted of cutlery, a small pot for cooking, and a tin cup.*

# Gumbo

*Gumbos were popular in the Southern states and tended to include anything which was on hand. Oysters were in abundance at this time and were not the delicacy they are today!*

1 large fish (codfish)
$1/4$ cup flour
Piece of butter size of an egg (4 Tbsps)
$1/2$ pound okra, sliced
12 oysters, shucked
Sassafras leaves, finely ground, or filé powder
Salt and pepper
Cayenne pepper

*Clean the fish and cut into chunks. Dredge the fish in flour and fry in the butter for a few minutes. Add the okra, cover with boiling water, and season. Simmer until the okra softens then add the oysters, ground sassafras leaves, salt and pepper, and cayenne pepper. Adjust seasoning if necessary and simmer for another five minutes. Serve with rice. Serves 4-6.*

### Rice Bread

*Boil six ounces of rice in a quart of water until it is dry and soft. Put it into two pounds of flour, mix it in well, add two teaspoons salt, two large spoons of yeast and as much water as will make it the consistency of bread. When well risen, bake in molds.*

Left: Southern refugees encamped in the woods near Vicksburg eagerly scan papers for any news of loved ones.

# Beef Stew

At the beginning of the war, Southern sympathizers would gladly share their meal with soldiers and certainly a home-cooked Beef Stew would be a welcome respite for soldiers starved of variety in their diet.

2 pounds beef
2 carrots, chopped
2 sticks celery, chopped
2 onions, sliced
4 potatoes, roughly chopped
Salt and pepper

Cut the beef into cubes and lay about half of it in the bottom of a saucepan. Mix half the carrot and celery through the beef then put a layer of onions and potatoes over the beef and season. Mix the remaining carrot and celery through the other half of the beef and lay this on top of the potatoes and onions. Top the stew off with a layer of potatoes and onion, season again, just cover with water, sprinkle with herbs and simmer for about $1^{1}/_{2}$ hours. Adjust seasoning before serving.

## Philadelphia Calf's Feet Jelly

Take a set of calf's feet and after cleaning, boil them in four quarts of water for five hours, skimming carefully. Strain through a colander, and set aside to cool. When cold, remove all the fat from the jelly.
Put the jelly into a saucepan with three or four sticks of cinnamon, three whole cloves, and the rind and juice of three lemons. Set on the fire.
Beat the whites and shells of four eggs in half a pint of cold water, stir in quickly with half a pound of white sugar dissolved in one pint of best "champagne cider" and a pint of sherry wine. Let it simmer for five minutes, set aside to settle, and pour through a jelly bag into molds to cool.

*When soldiers had a little money in their pockets, they treated themselves to an evening out by going to hotels and restaurants. The menu could vary widely, and was often no better than the rations in camp.*

*Right: the Union Volunteer Refreshment Saloon, near the railway in Philadelphia, fed an enormous number of Union soldiers. Below: most of the larger utensils would have been used by the camp kitchen, or shared between a number of men, as they soon learned to carry as little as possible with them.*

# Omelet Souffle

*This delicious dessert has very few ingredients and is very simple to make.*

6 eggs
6 Tbsps confectioners' sugar
Grated orange or lemon rind
Piece of butter size of an egg (4 Tbsps)

*Separate the eggs. Add the confectioners' sugar and grated orange/lemon rind to the egg yolks and blend until the mixture begins to turn white. Beat the egg whites with a whisk until they form stiff peaks and fold this into the yolk mixture. Melt the butter in a pan, pour in the omelet mixture and stir until the butter is absorbed by the egg mixture. Lightly butter a small oven-proof dish, pour in the omelet, sprinkle the top with powdered sugar and bake in a very hot oven until it has just started to turn light brown.*
*Serves 2.*

*Right: a woodcut dated 1864 illustrates the post-office at the Brooklyn Fair, in aid of the Sanitary Commission.*

58

*John Jackman of the 9th Kentucky Infantry went into Canton, Mississippi, on June 29, 1862, and bought a meal ticket at the local hotel, then crowded into the jammed dining hall and sat down. "Was fortunate enough to get a plate," he wrote, "and commenced bawling at a waiter to bring something to eat." He did not get his roast beef for some time. "At last it came, and though I always considered my teeth good, I could not even make a print on the piece brought me." Unable to get anything else brought to him, he joined the throng of other soldiers who took matters into their own hands and mobbed the kitchen. "There I found a crowd of soldiers, with plates in their hands, standing around the cook, who was preparing the last thing in the house fit to eat – a beef heart. My heart failed me," lamented Jackman, "and I went back to the train, and dined out of my haversack."*

*Right: excessive drinking was a common problem in both armies and this early picture was one of series of posed photographs showing the men becoming more and more inebriated.*

*Below: this illustration from the period shows a soldier preparing himself a frugal meal. Soldiers were forced to use their initiative to produce even the most basic meal, and their habit of frying everything in grease did not help the end result!*

# Cookies

*This cookie recipe has been slightly updated for today's tastes. During the war the number of ingredients available decreased and so many recipes became shorter and less tasty as the war progressed!*

*1 cup butter*
*2 cups sugar*
*³/4 cup milk*
*5 cups flour*
*1 tsp baking powder*
*Nutmeg to taste*

*Mix the butter and sugar together thoroughly and add the milk. Mix together the flour, baking powder, and nutmeg, and gradually add this to the butter mixture; mix well. Shape into balls, flatten each one and bake for about 20 minutes in a moderately hot oven (375° F). Makes about 30 cookies.*

# CHAPTER FOUR

# A Box from Home

*Above: Confederate camp, Warrington Navy Yard, Pensacola, Florida.*

*Throughout the war, families and friends back at home sent packages, boxes, even trunks, to their men in the armies. The welcome arrivals in camp came packed with home-made goodies like butter, preserves, pickles, smoked and cured joints, hams or fowl, tinned goods, especially condensed milk and berries, and fruits like apples and pears that would not perish on the journey. There were also nuts, cheeses, fruit pies, especially apple and cherry, and even cakes, the latter of the heavy fruit cake variety that could stand the rough trip to the front and last for weeks or months, thanks to a heavy lacing with rum or brandy. It was no easy task for people on the homefront to do this, especially in the Confederacy, where transportation by mail or express carrier was a chancy affair.*

Left: officers of the Washington Light Infantry, Charleston, South Carolina.

## Plum Cake

*Heavy, alcohol-laden cakes were the most suitable for surviving the long and arduous journey necessary to get boxes of gifts to the soldiers.*

5 cups all-purpose flour
2 cups sugar
1/2 tsp salt
1 tsp ground clove
1 tsp cinnamon
1 cup molasses
1/2 cup shortening
1 cup of butter
1 tsp soda
1 cup soured milk
2 Tbsps brandy
1/2 pound raisins, chopped
1/2 pound currants, chopped

*Mix the flour, sugar, salt, and spices together. Melt shortening, butter, and molasses, and mix into dry ingredients. Mix the soda in the sour milk and add to the mixture along with the brandy. Add the fruit and beat thoroughly. Pour into a large baking pan and bake in a low oven (325° F) for 2 1/2 hours.*

# Cherry Pie

*Pastry, or paste as it was then called, was used in both sweet and savory dishes to add bulk and flavor to a very plain filling.*

1 pound cherries, pitted
1/4 cup sugar

1/2 cup butter
2 cups flour
Pinch salt
Cold water

*To make the paste, rub the butter into the flour, add the salt and mix in enough cold water to make a nice dough. Roll out enough dough to fill a pie plate. Line the plate with the dough, fill with the cherries, and sprinkle with the sugar. Roll out the remaining dough and use to cover the cherry filling. Glaze with beaten egg, make a hole in the middle of the paste and bake the pie in a hot oven (400° F) until the pastry is a lovely light brown – about 30 minutes. Serves 4-6.*

*S*ome tried to send bread to their sons, but even that was unobtainable at times. In Richmond three different sized loaves sold for, respectively, one, two, and three dollars apiece. "The first is only visible by microscopick [sic] aid," wrote a cynical observer, "the second can be discerned with the naked eye, and the third can be seen with outline and shape intact."

*Below: a typical officer's mess chest began the war well stocked with plates, cutlery, a coffee boiler and canisters for sugar and salt. As the war progressed the chest and its contents would inevitably become shabby.*

*Left: although sutlers supplied many of the soldiers' requirements, their methods led many to be accused of racketeering.*

# Raspberry Jam

*This would have been greatly appreciated by men who were often starved of sweet foods and, of course, jam kept very well on its journey to camp.*

2 pounds firm, ripe raspberries
2 pounds sugar
Juice of ¹/₂ a lemon

*Rinse the fruit and place in a large saucepan, add the lemon juice and simmer until the fruit is soft and pulpy. Add the sugar and boil for about 3 minutes. Test the jam after this time by lifting a little out of the pot with a wooden spoon; if a blob of jelly forms the jam has reached setting point. This recipe should make about 3 jars.*

66

*Right: Lieutenant J.B. Neill of the 153rd New York. Facing page: the Western & Atlantic Railroad shed in Atlanta, which was destroyed by Sherman when he evacuated the city.*

# Sauerkraut

*This was a popular recipe in the North during the Civil War as it was believed to prevent scurvy, an illness soldiers were prone to because of their poor diet.*

Cabbage
Salt

*Wash the cabbage, cut into into quarters and remove the core. Shred the cabbage finely with a sharp knife. Place a layer of cabbage in a wide-mouthed jar or crock, sprinkle with salt and press down firmly. Continue this process until the jar is full. Cover the top with a clean cloth, put a plate on top and add a weight to weigh it down. Place the jar in a warm place to ferment. After a few days remove the froth which has formed on the top, replace the cloth, plate and weight and allow to stand for another three days, then repeat process. The jar should now be moved to a cool place. It will be ready in about 2 weeks.*

## Chocolate Candy

*This original recipe is from a receipt book of the time. It would have been a lucky soldier who received such a treat in his box from home.*

*Half a pound of chocolate, one and a half pounds of brown sugar, three quarters of a cup of milk. Grate the chocolate and mix with sugar and a little water. Put on the milk, and just before it boils stir in the mixture and boil till thick. Try a small quantity in a glass of water. If it hardens quickly it has boiled sufficiently.*

*A long with the goodies came new shirts, freshly made socks, maybe a blanket, candles, soap, and reading material. Indeed, one of the chief sources of books and magazines for soldiers was their friends and relatives, and food for thought went hand-in-hand with food for the body in the needs of many. "We must have something to eat, and the papers to read," wrote Captain Oliver Wendell Holmes. "Everything else we can do without," he said "only bread and newspapers we must have."*

*Right: this unidentified photograph of soldiers in camp gives a surprisingly relaxed image of the men enjoying a meal.*

# Beaten Biscuits

*These biscuits use the most basic of ingredients, which the baker would at least stand some chance of getting hold of.*

2 cups flour
$^1/_2$ tsp salt
1 Tbsp sugar
$^1/_4$ cup shortening
$^1/_2$ cup ice water

*Mix the flour, salt and sugar together. Cut in the shortening and add enough ice water to make a stiff dough. Beat the dough with a mallet until smooth, folding frequently. This takes about 20 minutes. Roll out the dough, cut with a small cookie cutter and bake for about 30 minutes in a moderate oven (375° F). If desired dust with confectioners' sugar. Makes about 20 small cookies.*

## Soap

*Soap was greatly treasured by the soldiers who were always pleased by its inclusion in their box from home. There were numerous different ways of producing soap; this fascinating receipt (recipe) is from a cookbook of the period.*

*Put on the fire any quantity of lye you choose that is strong enough to bear an egg – to each gallon, add three quarters of a pound of clean grease. Boil it very fast and stir it frequently – a few hours will suffice to make it good soap. When you find by cooling a little on a plate that it is a thick jelly, and no grease appears, put in salt in the proportion of one pint to three gallons – let it boil a few minutes – and pour it in tubs to cool. Next day, cut out the soap, melt it and cool it again; this takes out all the lye and keeps the soap from shrinking when dried.*

70

# CHAPTER FIVE

# Holiday Cookery

Above: McClellan's soldiers outside a sutler's store at Yorktown.

*"December 24, 1864*
*Raccoon Ford, Virginia*

*The night was excessively cold and we passed the evening in toasting our toes before a roaring fire – talking of home and the dear ones there in anything but a joyous strain ... We had made up our mind to go egg-nogless to bed, when – about 11 o'clock – the welcome sound of horses hoofs on the crisp snow outside; out we rushed and there we found the tardy 'Mose' with his well-filled demijohn. The eggs were quickly beaten – the sugar stirred in and then the whiskey added, and we had one of the most delicious nogs that ever that ever mortal man quaffed. Taking a couple of glasses a piece, we retired merrily to bed – to forget the hardships of a soldier's life, and dream of a joyful reunion with the dear absent ones far away in southland."*

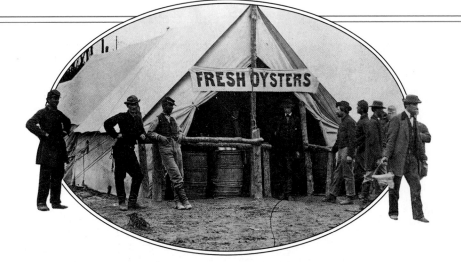

# Roast Turkey and Oyster Sauce

## Egg Nog

The recipe below for egg nog would have indeed been a special treat for a soldier even at Christmas. Unfortunately, they often had to make do with a far less rich mixture.

4 egg yolks
4 Tbsps sugar
1 cup cream (whipping)
1 cup brandy
1/4 cup wine
4 egg whites
A little grated nutmeg

Beat the egg yolks until light then slowly beat in the sugar, cream, brandy and wine. Whip the egg whites separately and then fold into the other ingredients. Sprinkle with the nutmeg to serve.

During the war, Christmas meant a desperate struggle for both soldiers and citizens to find something special for the occasion. Turkeys were of the wild variety, not the rather bland birds of today, and oysters were an everyday ingredient.

1 large turkey
Butter
10 oysters, shucked
1½ cups milk
Piece of butter size of an egg (4 Tbsps)
½ cup flour
Salt and pepper
1 Tbsp herbs

Wrap the turkey in aluminum foil and roast in a moderate oven (350° F) for 20 minutes per pound, plus 20 minutes. Remove the foil about 20 minutes before the end of cooking and brush the skin of the turkey with butter. Return the bird to the oven for the final cooking period. Meanwhile, strain the oysters and mix the juice with the milk; set aside. Melt the butter slowly, remove from heat, add the flour, and return to a gentle heat for a minute. Slowly stir in the milk mixture, stirring constantly. When the sauce has thickened and the turkey is almost ready to be served, add the oysters, seasoning, and herbs to the sauce and simmer just enough to heat the oysters. Serve the turkey ready for carving with the sauce alongside. Serves 10-12.

Above left: surprising as it may seem today, oysters were once readily available and not something a soldier would have considered a special treat.

*Captain William Seymour of the Confederacy's famed "Louisiana tigers," spoke for many in Blue and Gray when he recorded in his diary the hopes, disappointments, and simple pleasures of a soldier's Christmas. For the men in the ranks it was the premier holiday of the year. Union soldiers, always better supplied, often had festive holidays with their mess tables or camp kettles groaning with turkeys, chickens, hams, and special issues of vegetables, supplemented by goodies sent from home and goods locally purchased from sutlers and farmers.*

*Right: there was neither the nutritional knowledge nor the means to treat carcasses hygienically, and as a result much of the meat was practically inedible.*

*Below: soldiers occasionally managed to forget the war for a few hours and indulge in lighthearted games.*

# Beef Steaks

*Traditionally these steaks would have been cooked over an open fire, and if you have the opportunity to cook steaks in this manner don't miss it!*

*2 Tbsps butter or oil*
*2 beef steaks (best quality available)*
*3 onions*
*Black pepper*
*Mixed herbs*
*Fresh horseradish*

*Beat the steaks with a mallet. Peel the onions and cut into thick circles. Heat the butter or oil in a large frying pan, when hot place the steaks in the center of the pan and surround with the onion slices. Sprinkle the steaks and onions with the pepper and herbs and fry quickly over a high heat to required doneness, turning halfway through. When the steaks are almost ready, sprinkle over some grated horseradish. Serve the steaks straight from the pan. Serves 2.*

66**M**y Christmas dinner was bean soup without bread," a Reb wrote in his diary of December 25, 1863. "The boys are not seeing a good deal of fun." A year later it was only marginally better, with only fresh pork, baked sweet potatoes, hardtack, and a cold rain. "Bad prospect for a Christmas dinner," concluded Johnny Jackman of the 9th Kentucky.

*Right: cockfighting provides a distraction for the soldiers at General O.B. Willcox's headquarters, in front of Petersburg, August, 1864. Below: a comic representation of soldiers foraging for food.*

*Below: a few of Confederate general Robert E. Lee's personal military effects.*

# Sweet Potato Pudding

*Sweet potatoes were a common crop in the Southern states and often found their way into sweet dishes when no other alternatives were available.*

*6 medium-sized sweet potatoes
(white or orange-fleshed)
1 cup milk
1 cup sugar
3 eggs
Juice of a lemon
1 tsp cinnamon*

*Boil the potatoes for 30 minutes until soft and mash with the milk to a smooth consistency. Add the sugar, eggs, lemon juice, and cinnamon, and beat until smooth. Pour into a shallow, lightly buttered dish and bake in a moderate oven (375° F) for 30 minutes.
Serves 4.*

*Besides Christmas, men in both armies celebrated New Year in some fashion, and even the Fourth of July, for men North and South both looked back to the revolution with pride, though Confederates rarely honored the day after 1863, when the defeat at Gettysburg on July 3 was punctuated by the July 4 surrender of Vicksburg.*

*Above right: this illustration of a Thanksgiving ball shows that people tried to adhere to the ritual of normal life in spite of the war.*

# Gingerbread

*Gingerbread was very popular at this time, but all too often the taste of the bread depended on how many ingredients the cook could obtain for the recipe. This updated version brings together the best of the traditional ingredients alongside a few modern ones.*

*1 pound flour*
*1 level tsp each of salt and baking soda*
*1 level Tbsp each of ground ginger and baking powder*
*1 cup light brown sugar*
*³/₄ cup butter*
*¹/₂ cup each of molasses and corn syrup*
*1 generous cup of milk*
*1 egg, beaten*

*Grease and line a 9-inch square cake pan. Sift the flour, salt, baking soda, ginger, and baking powder into a large mixing bowl. In a saucepan, warm together the sugar, butter, molasses, and syrup until melted, but do not allow to boil. Mix in the milk and beaten egg. Make a well in the center of the dry ingredients, quickly pour in the liquid, and mix thoroughly. Pour the mixture into the pan and bake in a moderate oven (325° F) for 1¹/₂ hours, or until the gingerbread is light to the touch.*

*Right: winter quarters provided a comfortable and restful period for these officers enjoying simple pleasures such as reading and smoking.*

### Yankee Doughnuts

*Dry half a pound of good brown sugar, pound it, mix it with two pounds of flour and sift it. Add two spoonfuls of yeast, and as much new milk as will make it like bread. When well risen, knead in half a pound of butter, make it in cakes the size of half a dollar, and fry them to a light brown in hot oil.*

At least the summer holiday allowed a better chance of getting fresh fruit and vegetables from the seasonal crops. The later fall holiday of Thanksgiving was not then an official institution. Both sides called occasional days of "Thanksgiving and Prayer," but these were more often suggested as times for fasting and sacrifice than celebration and dining. For the men in the ranks, unfortunately, fasting and sacrifice were all too common already.

*Right and below: the Irish Brigade celebrates St. Patrick's Day with horse and mule races in the camp at Falmouth.*

*Below: a detail of General Lee's field quarters, showing his saddle and riding boots, among other accoutrements of war.*

# Pound Cake

As the war progressed and many items became scarce, cakes were often only made for holidays and special occasions. The extravagant (by Civil War standards) recipe below using nine eggs and brandy, is typical of cakes baked in the most affluent of homes for a homecoming or wedding party.

2 cups softened butter
2 cups sugar
9 eggs
4 cups flour
A pinch of salt
Grated lemon peel
A little grated nutmeg
1/2 cup brandy

Mix the butter and sugar together well and beat in the eggs. Sift the flour and salt together and mix in to the butter mixture until thoroughly blended. Add the lemon peel, nutmeg, and brandy, mix well and pour into two small buttered loaf pans or one large one. Bake in a moderate oven (350° F) for about 1 hour.

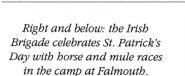

# On the Waters

*Above: gunners on the* USS Hunchback *loading a Dahlgren Howitzer, in 1864-65.*

"The food they had to eat was, at first, revolting to me," complained a midshipman in the Confederate Navy. "If it was not a tiny lump of fat pork, it was a shaving of fresh meat as tough as the hide which had once covered it, with a piece of hardtack and a tin cup of hot water colored by chicory or grains of burned corn, ground up and brevetted coffee."

*His was not the typical experience of navy food in the Civil War, for either side. Even in the Confederacy, seamen enjoyed a generally better quality and variety of victuals, thanks largely to their being stationed either beside rivers with abundant freshwater fish, or else near harbors and coastlines that provided seafood in abundance. One officer aboard the gunboat* Chattahoochee *told his father that he and his messmates ate "elegantly," enjoying "as elegant table as one would wish." Even whiskey and soda were occasionally consumed from glass tumblers aboard a warship, and champagne cocktails were not entirely unheard of. A paymaster aboard the Yankee ironclad USS Monitor declared "we have the best of food provided."*

*For the common seaman, the fare before him may not have been as varied or tasty as that in the officers' wardrooms, but still it was generally better than that endured by his counterparts in the armies.*

*Below: an 1864 pocket diary and watch belonging to an officer. Personal diaries give a fascinating and very emotive insight into the soldiers experience of war.*

*Above left: smoke from the cook's stove blows across the decks of the original Monitor. When not in action the crew took many of their meals on deck to avoid the sweltering heat below.*

# Traditional Baked Beans

*Beans were a common staple in the navy, and were often turned into quite respectable meals by the professional cooks who prepared meals for the men.*

1 pound navy beans
4oz salt pork
1 small onion, chopped
1 tsp dry mustard
½ cup molasses
Salt and pepper
1 cup water

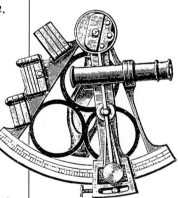

Cover the beans with water and soak overnight. Rinse, cover with fresh water and simmer for about 2 hours. Place the beans, salt pork, and onion in a casserole dish. Mix the mustard, molasses, salt, and pepper with the water and stir into the bean mixture. If the liquid does not just cover the beans, add a little water. Bake in a moderate oven (375° F) for about 2 hours. Remove the pork, break into pieces and return to the bean mixture before serving. Serves 6-8.

*Further to the wide variety of fish and seafood provided by the rivers and harbors, ships had designated cooks and stationary kitchens, modest though they were, that allowed for a better and more uniform grade of cookery.*

## Plum Duff

*This traditional pudding was a great favorite in the navy.*

½ oz fresh yeast
3 Tbsps light brown sugar
Water
2 cups flour
1 cup chopped plums
1 tsp nutmeg
Milk

Put the yeast and half the sugar in a bowl, add a few tablespoons of water, stir and leave to froth for a few minutes. Put the flour in a large bowl, make a well in the center and add the yeast mixture. Stir, and add enough water to make a stiff dough. Cover and set aside in a warm place to rise for two hours. After this time knock the dough back and add the plums, remaining sugar, nutmeg and enough milk to make the dough soft.

Tie the dough loosely in a cloth and put into a pot of boiling water. Cover and boil for about 1½ hours.

# Fish Chowder

*Civil War seamen had a better diet than their army counterparts. Stationed at ports or along coastlines, they had easier access to fresh seafood and any imported goods they could acquire.*

2 Tbsps oil
1 onion, chopped
Piece of salt pork
2 large fish ( cod or catfish)
$^1/_2$ pound potatoes, coarsely chopped
Salt and pepper
Piece of butter size of an egg (4 Tbsps)
$^1/_2$ cup flour
1 cup milk

Heat the oil and sauté the onion and salt pork; set aside. Clean the fish, cut into cubes and place in a pan with the potatoes and seasoning. Cover with water and simmer for about 15 minutes. In a separate pan slowly melt the butter, add the flour and cook for about a minute, remove from the heat and whip in the milk. Add the onion, salt pork, and white sauce to the fish and potatoes. Adjust seasoning, simmer for a few minutes and serve. Serves 4.

*Above left: a Confederate "David" torpedo boat, painted by Conrad Wise Chapman. The Davids could inflict serious damage by exploding charges against the hull of enemy vessels.*

# Chicken Pot Pie

Officers in the navy were amongst the luckiest in terms of their diet. They tended to have professional cooks and a good supply of ingredients, therefore almost anything could arrive on the wardroom table, and it was usually of a comparatively high standard.

1 chicken
Piece of butter size of an egg (4 Tbsps)
$^{1}/_{2}$ cup flour
3 carrots, sliced
2 onions, chopped
$^{1}/_{2}$ cup peas
Salt and pepper

2$^{1}/_{2}$ cups flour
$^{1}/_{2}$ tsp salt
2 eggs
Milk

Cut the chicken into pieces and place in a pan, cover with water and simmer for about 30 minutes. Remove the chicken from the pan; keep warm. Reserve the stock. Melt the butter in a saucepan and add the flour, heat gently for about 1 minute and gradually stir in enough of the chicken stock to make a sauce. Return the chicken to the sauce, pour into a casserole, season and add the remaining vegetables. Meanwhile, mix the flour with the salt, make a well in the center and add the eggs. Mix thoroughly and if the mixture is a little stiff, add some milk. Roll out the dough and place on top of the chicken stew. Cook the pie in a moderate oven (375° F) for about 30 minutes when the vegetables should be cooked through.

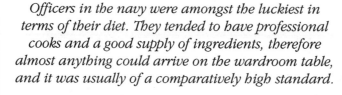

90

*Then there was the grog ration, a daily issue of rum or whiskey, watered down, but still intoxicating. When the Union Navy Department went through an abstemious streak and tried to abolish it, there was near-mutiny. Men would put up with something pretty tiresome on their plates, if there was something good in their mugs.*

*Right: stationed at ports and along rivers meant that the navy was better supplied than the army. Consequently naval officers could expect reasonably tasty meals in the wardroom.*

# Pumpkin Bread

*A great favorite in the South, pumpkin bread utilized the large pumpkin crop available in the early years of the war.*

2 eggs
1 cup of cooked pumpkin, mashed
2 cups flour
3/4 cup sugar
1/2 tsp grated nutmeg

*Mix the eggs and pumpkin together, then mix in the flour, sugar, and nutmeg. Fold together well and put into a well-buttered 9 x 5-inch loaf pan. Bake in a moderate oven (350° F) for about 1 hour.*

### Cherry Rum

*Sailors were given a daily grog ration, a treat not enjoyed by the soldiers. This traditional recipe is a lot grander than the ration the men would receive.*

*A peck of black wild cherries, soaked in cold water for twenty four hours. Put them in a demijohn, add two pounds brown sugar, two quarts blackberries, and a gallon of best New England rum. The older it is the better, if kept well corked.*

# Index

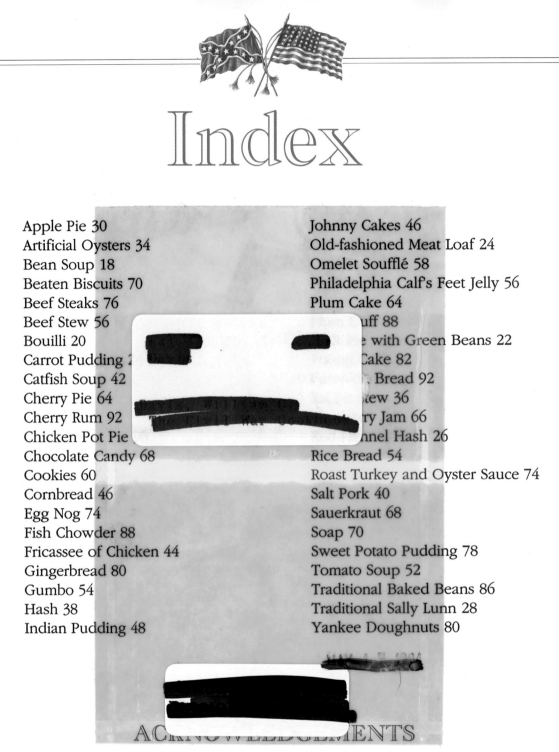

ACKNOWLEDGEMENTS

The publishers would like to thank the following organizations and individuals for the use of their illustrations in this book: The Bettmann Archive; The New York Historical Society; Library of Congress; National Archives; Kean Archives, Philadelphia; T. Scott Sanders Collection; Alvan C. Macauley, Michigan; Dale S. Snair, Richmond, Virginia; Lloyd Ostendorf Collection; William C. Davis; Tria Giovan